READ-ALOUD PLAYS

REVOLUTIONARY WAR

by

Dallas Murphy

SCHOLASTIC
PROFESSIONAL BOOKS

New York • Toronto • London • Auckland • Sydney
Mexico City • New Delhi • Hong Kong

Cover design by Jaime Lucero
Interior design by Melinda Belter
Cover art and interior illustrations by Mona Mark

ISBN: 0-590-03325-5

Printed in the U.S.A.

TABLE
OF
CONTENTS

INTRODUCTION

WHO WERE THE AMERICAN COLONISTS and why did they rebel against King George and Parliament during the American Revolution? What was their fight for independence from England all about? How have the events of this period impacted American life today?

Read-Aloud Plays: Revolutionary War invites students to explore the revolutionary characters, pivotal events, and critical issues of this formative period in American history. These five original plays present an overview of the American Revolution—its roots in the Boston Massacre and the Boston Tea Party, the division that existed between Patriots and Loyalists, and two major American victories at Trenton and at Yorktown, which signaled the end of the long war.

Description of the Teaching Guides

This collection of plays and supporting materials are designed to enrich your existing social studies curriculum. Each play is followed by background information on the event, a bibliography of fiction and nonfiction books, and six related activities. The activities emphasize critical thinking about historical issues through discussion, writing, and researching. They promote individual work as well as cooperative learning. Feel free to adjust the activity plans to meet the particular needs and interests of your students.

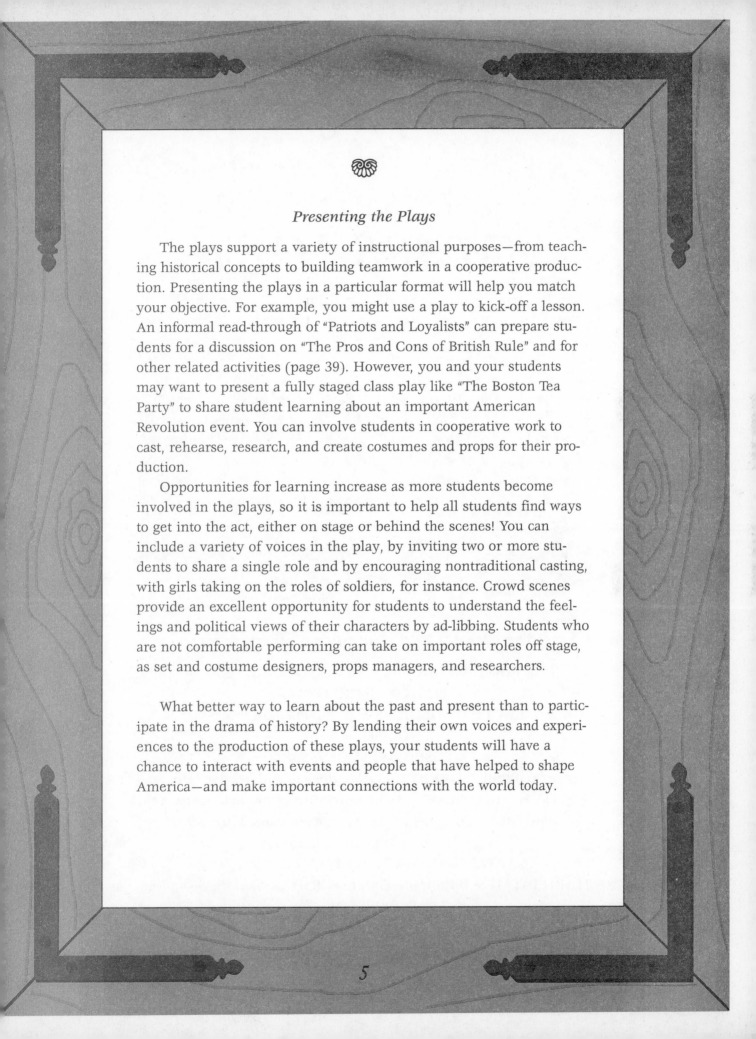

Presenting the Plays

The plays support a variety of instructional purposes—from teaching historical concepts to building teamwork in a cooperative production. Presenting the plays in a particular format will help you match your objective. For example, you might use a play to kick-off a lesson. An informal read-through of "Patriots and Loyalists" can prepare students for a discussion on "The Pros and Cons of British Rule" and for other related activities (page 39). However, you and your students may want to present a fully staged class play like "The Boston Tea Party" to share student learning about an important American Revolution event. You can involve students in cooperative work to cast, rehearse, research, and create costumes and props for their production.

Opportunities for learning increase as more students become involved in the plays, so it is important to help all students find ways to get into the act, either on stage or behind the scenes! You can include a variety of voices in the play, by inviting two or more students to share a single role and by encouraging nontraditional casting, with girls taking on the roles of soldiers, for instance. Crowd scenes provide an excellent opportunity for students to understand the feelings and political views of their characters by ad-libbing. Students who are not comfortable performing can take on important roles off stage, as set and costume designers, props managers, and researchers.

What better way to learn about the past and present than to participate in the drama of history? By lending their own voices and experiences to the production of these plays, your students will have a chance to interact with events and people that have helped to shape America—and make important connections with the world today.

1770
The
BOSTON
MASSACRE

The CHARACTERS (in order of appearance)

FIRST NARRATOR • SECOND NARRATOR

BOSTON CITIZENS 1–8

ENGLISH SOLDIERS 1–8 (*nonspeaking roles*)

ENGLISH SENTRY

CRISPUS ATTUCKS: *Sailor*

LORD GEORGE GRENVILLE: *Member of English Parliament*

LORD CHARLES TOWNSHEND: *Member of English Parliament*

MEMBERS OF PARLIAMENT 1–8 (*nonspeaking roles*)

JOHN GREY: *Boston shopkeeper*

CAPTAIN THOMAS PRESTON: *English officer*

RICHARD PALMES: *Boston merchant* • JOHN ADAMS: *Boston lawyer*

NEWSBOY

Act 1

THE TIME AND PLACE
March 5, 1770; Boston, Massachusetts

THE SETTING
Outside the Customs House

FIRST NARRATOR: The American Revolution might have never happened. Not everyone in the 13 American colonies wanted independence, and almost no one imagined that the colonists, who had no standing army and no navy, could defeat the strongest military power in the world since the Roman Empire.

SECOND NARRATOR: And when we look back across the centuries, great events of history sometimes seem neat and orderly, planned out in advance, but many times the small events that led to great ones were disorderly and accidental. The Boston Massacre was one of those.

FIRST NARRATOR: Neither side meant for there to be bloodshed that day—

SECOND NARRATOR: March 5, 1770—

FIRST NARRATOR: In Boston, Massachusetts.

SECOND NARRATOR: A wet snow had fallen overnight—

FIRST NARRATOR: Perfect for making snowballs.

SECOND NARRATOR: Look. A crowd is gathering around the Customs House.

FIRST NARRATOR: That is where the money from the hated taxes is stored.

SECOND NARRATOR: A single sentry stands guard.

CITIZEN 1: Lobsterback!

CITIZEN 2: Go home, lobsterback!

FIRST NARRATOR: They called the British soldiers lobsterbacks because of their red coats.

SECOND NARRATOR: In those days, lobsters weren't considered a delicacy. Lobsters were everywhere along the shore, and in minutes, you could pick up more than you could carry. Only the very poor people ate them, and others used them for fertilizer.

CITIZEN 3: The British are thieves!

CITIZEN 4: Tyrants!

CITIZEN 5: Invaders!

CITIZEN 6: Tar and feather them!

CITIZEN 7: Lobsterbacks!

FIRST NARRATOR: Actually, the common British soldier wanted to be friendly with the American colonists.

SECOND NARRATOR: The British soldiers did not want to be here, so far away from their homes, but the colonists saw them as an occupying army, which they were.

FIRST NARRATOR: It was an impossible situation.

SECOND NARRATOR: The current of events was moving too quickly for anyone to control.

SENTRY: Go away, you thugs!

CITIZEN 8: Thugs? He calls *us* thugs?

CRISPUS ATTUCKS: If *we* had invaded London, then he might rightly call us thugs!

FIRST NARRATOR: Uh-oh, now they're starting to throw snowballs at the sentry.

CITIZEN 1: Down with British tyranny!

ATTUCKS: Down with the Townshend Acts!

SECOND NARRATOR: See that man who just shouted "Down with the Townshend Acts!"? That's Crispus Attucks, a black sailor.

FIRST NARRATOR: Most of the facts about his life have been lost in time, but he's about to pay a big price for his views.

SECOND NARRATOR: The Townshend Acts provoked all this.

FIRST NARRATOR: The Townshend Acts were import duties, in other words, taxes on goods imported from England.

SECOND NARRATOR: England taxed goods such as paper, glass, paint, and tea. The colonists didn't object to paying *all* taxes. Every English person paid taxes. It's just that the colonists wanted to be consulted about it.

FIRST NARRATOR: The men who wanted independence—patriots such as Sam Adams, Paul Revere, and Ben Franklin—needed a cause around which to rally the people to their side. Lofty talk and beautiful language about the rights of people wouldn't do it. They needed something concrete, something everyone could understand. With the Townshend Acts, the British handed the patriots a cause.

SECOND NARRATOR: Coincidentally, there was a political battle going on back in England between two competing parties, and one party used the issue of colonial taxes to taunt the other side. Neither really cared about the issue itself, but they should have.

FIRST NARRATOR: To see how this happened, let's shift the scene back to the English Parliament in London.

Act 2

THE TIME AND PLACE
1767; London, England

THE SETTING
Inside the English Parliament

LORD GRENVILLE: You're cowards. You're afraid of the Americans. "We dare not tax America!" you whine.

The members of Parliament mutter to each other. Some nod their heads in agreement. Others shake their heads violently to disagree.

SECOND NARRATOR: That was Lord Grenville. He used to be the head of Parliament, sort of like our president, but he got voted out of office, and now he wants to gain it back.

LORD TOWNSHEND: Do I fear Americans? No. Am I a coward? Dare I not tax America? I dare! I am no coward! I dare to tax America!

FIRST NARRATOR: And that was Lord Townshend. He's like our secretary of the treasury.

GRENVILLE: Do you, Townshend? I wish to God I could see it!

TOWNSHEND: By God, you will see it!

SECOND NARRATOR: It's interesting to wonder what might have happened if the British had behaved more diplomatically, more intelligently toward her colonies in America. But colonies, especially those so far away, were expensive to maintain. Lord Grenville, looking for a cause to help him get reelected, found a popular one in the idea that the colonies should help pay for their keep. It wasn't a smart move, but Lord Townshend jumped at it.

FIRST NARRATOR: That led straight to trouble—and back to Boston.

Act 3

THE TIME AND PLACE
March 5, 1770; Boston, Massachusetts

THE SETTING
Outside the Customs House

SECOND NARRATOR: As you can see, the angry crowd has grown.

CITIZEN 2: Tar and feather Lord Townshend!

SENTRY: That shows what you know! Lord Townshend's been dead these three years

CITIZEN 3: Good!

CITIZEN 4: May he rot!

CITIZEN 5: May all England rot!

SENTRY: Stop throwing things, you rabble, or I'll shoot in self-defense!

ATTUCKS: Defense? We're the ones who need defense! Against you!

SECOND NARRATOR: Here comes John Grey—

JOHN GREY: Break it up! Everyone, go home.

FIRST NARRATOR: John Grey owns that rope-making shop over there. Many merchants were against independence because they thought it would be bad for business.

GREY: Go home, I say. Leave that sentry alone or there will be trouble!

CITIZEN 6: You've got some nerve, John Grey!

CITIZEN 7: He's been hiring British soldiers at the expense of Americans.

CITIZEN 8: Shame on you, John Grey!

CITIZEN 1: You're a traitor, Grey!

SENTRY: He's not a traitor. You're the traitors—you've betrayed England and your king!

ATTUCKS: Tar and feather King George!

SENTRY: Hey, you, watch your mouth!

ATTUCKS: Down with England!

GREY: Break it up! Break it up, I say!

SECOND NARRATOR: They're throwing snowballs again.

FIRST NARRATOR: And rocks.

SECOND NARRATOR: Here comes an officer.

FIRST NARRATOR: It's Thomas Preston, captain of the guard.

PRESTON: Disperse, you troublemakers, disperse at once or I'll call out the guard!

ATTUCKS: Look, he's drawing his sword. He means to attack us!

SECOND NARRATOR: A rock hits the captain—

FIRST NARRATOR: Now it's going to turn serious—

GREY: Stop this!

CITIZEN 2: Go back and supervise your British soldiers!

CITIZEN 3: They're probably loafing—

PRESTON: Send in the guard!

SECOND NARRATOR: Here they come! One, two, three . . . five . . . eight. Eight soldiers, and they're armed for battle. Captain Preston takes his place at the head of the line.

ATTUCKS: Why don't you fire? You don't dare fire on us!

RICHARD PALMES: Wait, Captain! Wait! I'm certain we can settle this without violence!

FIRST NARRATOR: That's Richard Palmes, a respected local merchant who tries to act as peacemaker.

SECOND NARRATOR: But it's too late for peace.

PALMES: Sir, I trust you mean no harm to these people.

CAPTAIN: By no means, sir. But we'll fire in self-defense, make no mistake about that.

CITIZEN 4: Put down your weapons and fight like men!

ATTUCKS: Cowards!

CAPTAIN: Step back, you people! Do not crowd us! You stand warned.

PALMES: Stop throwing things! Stop this now!

FIRST NARRATOR: But someone reaches out and grabs one of the soldier's muskets.

PALMES: No!

SECOND NARRATOR: The gun goes off!

FIRST NARRATOR: Then all the soldiers fire!

There are sound of gunfire, shouts, and screams. Attucks and other citizens fall down, wounded. Then all sound stops.

FIRST NARRATOR: It's happened, the first bloodshed, and the war hasn't even started.

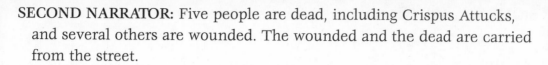

SECOND NARRATOR: Five people are dead, including Crispus Attucks, and several others are wounded. The wounded and the dead are carried from the street.

FIRST NARRATOR: Captain Preston seems panic-stricken. He didn't mean for this to happen, and he'll have to answer for it. He's marching his men away, screaming at them as the gun smoke fades in the cold winter breeze.

SECOND NARRATOR: But the story didn't end there.

Act 4

THE TIME AND PLACE
December 5, 1770; Boston, Massachusetts

THE SETTING
A courtroom

FIRST NARRATOR: Captain Preston and his men were placed on trial for murder. One of the most famous patriots, John Adams, volunteered to defend them.

CITIZEN 5: Are you out of your mind, Adams? Those men killed Americans in cold blood. How can you defend them?

JOHN ADAMS: I do it not because I love England, but because I love liberty. There can be no liberty if the right to a fair trial is denied to anyone.

SECOND NARRATOR: The soldiers were found guilty of manslaughter by a jury of Bostonians and given only token punishment. That was a fair verdict, because to be guilty of murder, you must have intended to kill a person.

FIRST NARRATOR: That wasn't the soldiers' intention, and besides, they were provoked by an angry crowd. Nobody in that crowd deserved to get shot, but without them—their words and actions—the incident would never have happened.

CITIZEN 6: I hope you're happy, Adams.

JOHN ADAMS: The truth, whether it serves our aims or not, is all that matters in the court of justice.

CITIZEN 7: John's right. How can we accuse the English of taking away our rights, and then turn around and do the same to their citizens?

SECOND NARRATOR: The radical patriot, Samuel Adams, agreed with his cousin John completely on everything—including the right to resist injustice and tyranny, the right of freedom.

FIRST NARRATOR: But Sam believed that to attain freedom, you sometimes needed to stretch the truth. He stretched it a lot. Let's move outside, and you'll see what I mean.

NEWSBOY: Read all about it. Murder! Redcoats murder the citizens of Boston! Get the latest by Sam Adams, eyewitness to massacre. INNOCENT BLOOD CRYING TO GOD FROM THE STREETS OF BOSTON, by Sam Adams. Get one while they last!

SECOND NARRATOR: Sam also encouraged his friend Paul Revere to engrave a picture of the shooting on a copper plate so that it could be printed on paper and widely distributed. It showed a line of British soldiers intentionally firing into a crowd of respectable unarmed citizens. This picture became the "truth" to most colonists. That's what propaganda is all about.

FIRST NARRATOR: Sam Adams was a true radical, but then the idea he and other Patriots believed in was also radical in those days. The idea was this: The general public should, and could, choose their own leaders.

SECOND NARRATOR: Oh, by the way, on March 5, 1770, the very day of the Boston Massacre, the English Parliament repealed the Townshend Acts. The good news about the taxes would reach American shores several weeks too late.

BACKGROUND
ON THE
BOSTON MASSACRE

ENGLAND VIEWED THE AMERICAN colonies as an economic offshoot. In 1651, the British Parliament passed the Navigation Acts: All goods going into the colonies from foreign countries had to first pass through English ports where customs fees would be collected; the colonies were forbidden to ship certain goods to any country but England. Some angry colonists defied the acts by smuggling goods in and out of America.

Then, in 1754, France moved into the Ohio Valley, which England considered its own territory. The French and Indian War broke out. Although England won, the war put the country heavily in debt. King George III reasoned that the American colonies should help pay that debt. He decreed that the Navigation Acts be strictly enforced. British soldiers were authorized to break into colonists' homes without search warrants to look for contraband goods. A force of 10,000 British soldiers was stationed in America. Under the Quartering Act of 1765, the colonists were required to house the soldiers in inns and other buildings.

King George III and Parliament also decided that colonists had to pay taxes on imported goods. The final straw came with the Stamp Act of 1765. Colonists had to buy government stamps to place on all legal documents, newspapers, insurance policies, and even playing cards. Because they weren't represented in Parliament, where they could vote on these issues, the Americans believed the act was a case of taxation without representation. Two groups, the Sons of Liberty and the Committees of Correspondence, sprang up throughout the colonies to fight the Stamp Act. Then taxes were levied on imported glass, lead, paper, and tea. The colonists refused to buy these items.

REVOLUTIONARY READING

The Boston Massacre (Famous Trials Series) by Bonnie L. Lukes (Lucent Books, 1998)

Crispus Attucks: Black Leader of Colonial Patriots by Dharathula H. Millender (Aladdin, 1986)

The Fifth of March: A Story of the Boston Massacre by Ann Rinaldi (Gulliver, 1994)

ACTIVITIES

Making Your Voice Heard

About which contemporary issues do students have strong feelings? How do, or would, they make their voices heard? Which methods—for example, letter writing, protesting, talking to friends and neighbors—do they feel would be most effective in getting their messages across?

A Taxing Question

Talk about the kinds of taxes people in your community pay, such as sales tax, state and federal income taxes, and property taxes. What items would students tax to raise money, and why?

News Travels . . . Slowly

Invite students to imagine how their worlds would be different without modern communication devices like telephones, fax machines, and electronic mail, or services like overnight mail delivery and international flights. Students might consider the methods of overseas communication available in the late 18th century and how this may have affected relations between King George and his Parliament and the colonists.

Dear King George

Encourage pairs of students to assume the roles of an American colonist and King George. The American colonist writes a letter to the English king expressing his or her views on the Navigation, Stamp, and Quartering Acts. The king then replies to the colonist, expressing his country's view of the colonies.

Slogans Instead of Snowballs

Suppose the Bostonians had carried signs with slogans on them instead of verbally taunting the British soldiers and then throwing snowballs at them. Ask students to create at least three different signs to show the colonists' discontent with the British soldiers, King George III, and Parliament.

Crispus Attucks Was . . .

Who was Crispus Attucks? Challenge students to find out more about this American patriot. Challenge them to present their findings in creative ways; for example, in the form of a plan for a short documentary or as a design for a Web page. What kinds of resource materials would they use—letters, maps, illustrations, oral histories, music, and so on?

John Adams: Traitor or Patriot?

John Adams defended the British soldiers who opened fire and killed the Boston citizens. Was he a traitor or a patriot? Direct students to research the trial. Then ask them to write a play about or a newspaper account of the trial, with the focus on John Adams's role. Students may work together in pairs or groups, or individually.

1773
The
BOSTON
TEA PARTY

The CHARACTERS (in order of appearance)

NARRATOR

FIRST MR. SMITH • SECOND MR. SMITH

BOSTON CITIZENS 1–8

MR. JONES

BRITISH SOLDIERS 1–2

GOVERNOR HUTCHINSON: *Governor of Massachusetts colony*

JOSIAH QUINCY: *Boston radical*

SONS OF LIBERTY 1–8

SAMUEL ADAMS: *Boston radical*

MESSENGER

BRITISH SENTRIES 1–2

Act 1

THE TIME AND PLACE
December 16, 1773; Boston, Massachusetts

THE SETTING
Tremont Street, Boston, Massachusetts

NARRATOR: Something's going to happen tonight. I don't know what, but you can feel the tension and excitement in the cold air. The streets of Boston, normally quiet on a winter evening, are crowded with people. Some are milling about, others are in small groups arguing among themselves, and still others are shouting anti-British slogans. Relations between England and the American colonies have been strained lately, and I hear people actually talking about revolution. Some say they're ready to fight for liberty.

Wait, here comes a man. Let's ask him what's going on. Sir, sir, excuse me, sir—

FIRST MR. SMITH: Yes, what is it?

NARRATOR: I wonder, sir, if you could tell me what's going on tonight?

SMITH: Who are you?

NARRATOR: I'm the narrator.

SMITH: Oh. Well, I'm in something of a rush—

NARRATOR: I wonder if you could tell me what's going on here tonight?

SMITH: Where?

NARRATOR: Here. On Tremont Street. Boston, Massachusetts. What's your name, sir?

SMITH: My name? Ah . . . Smith, Mr. Smith.

NARRATOR: I won't keep you, Mr. Smith, but could you tell me why these people are so angry?

SMITH: I would love to stay and talk, but I'm late for a meeting.

NARRATOR: A meeting? A political meeting? Are you a member of the Sons of Liberty?

SMITH: Sons of Liberty? Never heard of them. Now if you'll excuse me.

He hurries off. Another man approaches.

NARRATOR: Excuse me, sir, but I wonder if you could tell me what's happening here tonight.

SECOND MR. SMITH: Who are you?

NARRATOR: I'm the narrator.

SMITH: Oh. How do you do? I'm Mr. Smith.

NARRATOR: Smith? There are a lot of Smiths in Boston.

SMITH: As narrator, aren't you supposed to know everything?

NARRATOR: There are many different kinds of narrators.

SMITH: Haven't you heard of the tea tax?

NARRATOR: I've heard of it, but—

SMITH: The British are trying to punish us as though we were rude children. Well, we'll show—oh. The tea tax, yes. We were talking about the tea tax. Last summer, England passed the Tea Act. It gave the East India Company, a trade company, the right to determine who could sell tea in the colonies and who couldn't. Only those who profess loyalty to the Crown can sell tea. Since one million of we Colonists drink tea twice a day, that amounts to a lot of money. But that's not the main point. The main point is, if Parliament can control who sells tea, it can control who sells anything in the colonies.

NARRATOR: Then, Mr. Smith, sir, do you advocate a complete break with England?

SMITH: A complete break? Independence? Why, that would be treason. We're honorable people. England will come to her senses. We can work out our differences in an agreeable manner.

NARRATOR: I understand the Sons of Liberty are meeting tonight. Would you know anything about that?

SMITH: The Sons of Liberty? Oh. Let me see. Sounds familiar. Yes, isn't that a naturalist's club? They study birds, I believe, and butterflies.

NARRATOR: Actually, I believe it's a political organization.

SMITH: Politics? Oh. I don't follow politics. I'm merely a tea merchant.

NARRATOR: Tea? But, sir, didn't you just say that the tea tax was tyranny?

SMITH: Oh! Please excuse me. I have an appointment. With my blacksmith.

He walks off.

CITIZEN 1: Bloody Redcoats!

CITIZEN 2: Get off our shores!

CITIZEN 3: They're worse than Egyptian tyrants!

NARRATOR: Let's tag along behind Mr. Smith and see if we can learn anything more.

NARRATOR follows SECOND MR. SMITH to a building near the harbor. He goes in.

NARRATOR: What's this? A printer's shop. The Edes and Gillis Printing Office. I hear raised voices from upstairs inside. Let's see if we can—

MR. JONES: I'm sorry, but this is a private meeting. With all respect, you may not enter here.

NARRATOR: I'm the Narrator, and I was wondering if the Sons of Liberty were meeting here.

JONES: The Sons of Liberty? We're printers. We're discussing ink.

NARRATOR: What is your name, sir?

JONES: Uh . . . Jones. Mr. Jones. Now if you'll excuse me.

He closes the door.

CITIZEN 4: Down with the King!

CITIZEN 5: Down with England!

NARRATOR: Let's see if we can get the British viewpoint from Governor Hutchinson. The governor's residence is down this way, toward the harbor, only a five-minute walk. Wait, there are a couple of British soldiers over there in the shadows. Let's get their perspective. Good evening, officers.

SOLDIER 1: Here, now, we don't want no trouble.

NARRATOR: No, no trouble. I'd like to ask your opinions on the tea tax.

SOLDIER 2: Our opinion? You want *our* opinion?

NARRATOR: Why, yes.

SOLDIER 1: I don't think anybody ever asked us our opinion on anything.

SOLDIER 2: We're not officers. We're just common soldiers. Privates. Who are you?

NARRATOR: I'm the Narrator.

SOLDIER 2: And you want to know what we think of the tea tax? Well, we think it's unfair.

SOLDIER 1: That's right, but it's not really about tax or tea, is it, sir? We've been mulling it over. Look at it like this. These colonists already pay taxes. It's not like they're saying they won't pay any taxes at all.

SOLDIER 2: But the colonists have been acting uppity-like, saying they shouldn't be taxed if they don't have a vote on it in Parliament.

SOLDIER 1: You didn't hear this from me, but we agree with that. But the colonists? They're dreaming if they think King George is going to let them tell him what to do.

SOLDIER 2: Duck!

A rock hits the wall nearby.

SOLDIER 1: They're starting to throw stuff.

NARRATOR: Tell me, gentlemen, what are your orders?

SOLDIER 2: Our orders? Do nothing.

SOLDIER 1: Avoid trouble no matter what.

SOLDIER 2: Trouble is, if it comes down to violence, we're going to have to shoot these people even if we agree with them. Nobody's going to ask our opinions on it.

SOLDIER 1: Excuse us, we'd better move along.

They leave.

NARRATOR: Well, let's go on to Governor Hutchinson's house and hear what he has to say.

Act 2

THE SETTING
Governor Hutchinson's residence

HUTCHINSON: First of all, I do not represent the British viewpoint, as you put it. I am a Massachusetts man. I have steadfastly opposed the sterner measures taken by the Crown thus far, but you must remember one fact. We are all Englishmen, and as such we are subject to the laws of Parliament and the Crown. If we do not like those laws, then we may petition Parliament with our grievances. But in the meantime we must abide by them.

NARRATOR: Some colonists say they should not be taxed by Parliament since they have no leader to represent them in Parliament. "No taxation without representation," is how they put it. The Sons of Liberty are saying that taxation without representation is tyranny.

HUTCHINSON: The Sons of Liberty! Don't talk to me about the Sons of Liberty. They're radicals. Look out there, look at that mob. We have mobs on the streets of Boston, and they've been incited by the rabble-rousing talk of men like Samuel Adams, Josiah Quincy, and Thomas Paine. They're radicals, every one of those Sons of . . . Sons of Liberty. Their cause is treason.

NARRATOR: Don't the colonists have the right to—

HUTCHINSON: I'll tell you about rights. It's really quite simple. It boils down to this: We as Americans have no rights other than those that the king and Parliament choose to recognize. Do you know what those Sons of Liberty want me to do? I'll tell you. They've demanded that I send those three tea ships anchored in the harbor back to England. They *demand* that I do this as a protest against the Tea Act.

NARRATOR: Are you going to do it?

HUTCHINSON: I most assuredly am not. Those ships have already cleared customs. It would be against the law to make them leave now. British law. Now if you'll excuse me I have work to do even at this late hour. There's a mob on my streets.

Act 3

THE SETTING
Sons of Liberty meeting, back on Tremont Street

JOSIAH QUINCY: Are we going to sit here and do nothing?

SONS OF LIBERTY: No! Nay!

QUINCY: Are we going to sit by while tyrants heap insult on injury?

SONS OF LIBERTY: No!

QUINCY: No? Then what shall we do? Talk? Discuss? Debate?

SON OF LIBERTY 1: No!

SON OF LIBERTY 2: We'll act!

SON OF LIBERTY 3: We'll act this very night!

QUINCY: Do you know what they say about us in the South? In Charleston, where patriots unloaded the tyrant's tea into a damp warehouse and let it rot, they say, "Bostonians are better at resolving what to do than doing what they resolve."

SON OF LIBERTY 4: The time for talk has passed!

QUINCY: What do you say, Samuel Adams?

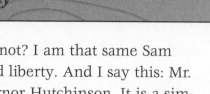

SAMUEL ADAMS: You all know me, do you not? I am that same Sam Adams who has opposed tyranny and loved liberty. And I say this: Mr. Quincy and I have sent a demand to Governor Hutchinson. It is a simple demand. It says: Return those tea ships to England. We are committed to this demand. However, we must wait until the governor replies. But know this. If we act, the tyrant will call our actions treason, and he will react accordingly.

SON OF LIBERTY 5: Sam, the messenger's just come from the governor's residence.

MESSENGER: Governor Hutchinson says he will not return the tea ships to England.

QUINCY: Did he say nothing else?

MESSENGER: Nothing.

ADAMS: Gentlemen, this meeting can do nothing further to save the country.

Act 4

THE SETTING
Boston streets

NARRATOR: What's this! Indians? Mohawk Indians coming from the print shop? That couldn't be . . . .They're carrying clubs and tomahawks, and they're—no, they're white men in disguise. They've darkened their faces with soot. They're hurrying down Tremont Street. Something is going to happen. Sir, sir, what's going on here?

SON OF LIBERTY 6: Step aside, step aside. We have no time to talk now.

NARRATOR: But why are you dressed like that?

SON OF LIBERTY 7: We're going to see how the King's tea mixes with salt water.

NARRATOR: What? Salt water? You mean—wait! Other men in disguise are joining from the side streets. They're heading for the harbor. I wonder . . . .Sir, excuse me, sir, do you intend to attack the tea ships?

SON OF LIBERTY 8: We're unarmed, as you can see.

NARRATOR: But you have hatchets and clubs.

SON OF LIBERTY 1: We mean no harm to any man.

SON OF LIBERTY 2: We mean harm to King George's tea.

NARRATOR: They're running now. I'll try to keep up. Oh, no! There's an armed sentry at the head of Griffith's Wharf, and he's leveled his musket. Is there going to be violence?

SENTRY 1: Halt! Who are you men? What do you want?

SON OF LIBERTY 3: We want nothing from you.

SON OF LIBERTY 4: We ask you to step aside. We want no bloodshed, but as you can see, you are far outnumbered. Please step aside.

NARRATOR: Everyone is tense. What's going to happen? Wait—the sentry has lowered his rifle. He's letting the men pass. Now they're boarding the ship. They actually mean to do this—there's another sentry on deck!

SENTRY 2: Halt! You may not board here.

SON OF LIBERTY 5: A good evening to you, sir. As you can plainly see, you are outnumbered, and since we mean you no harm, we request you lower your musket and let us get on with our business.

SENTRY 2: Your business is treason, sir.

SON OF LIBERTY 6: So it is, but we will conduct it.

SENTRY 2: If you damage the ship, my captain will not go easy on me.

SON OF LIBERTY 6: Sir, if I had time, I would polish her binnacle.

NARRATOR: They're all going aboard now. I think I know what they're going to do . . . .Yes. They're throwing bales of tea over the side into the harbor. They're sweeping the decks clean. It's a strange sight this night in Boston. A king's ship seized by men dressed as Mohawks—I can see them on deck outlined against the pale winter moon—as hundreds of pounds of tea drift away on the tide.

Well, there you have it, ladies and gentlemen. The Sons of Liberty are climbing back to Griffith's Wharf and dispersing in all directions. If there is war, and in it the colonists win their independence, then we will have witnessed history in the making. In any case, King George cannot ignore this affront. Something will surely happen now, but only time will tell its outcome.

BACKGROUND
ON THE
BOSTON TEA PARTY

WHEN KING GEORGE III and Parliament passed the Stamp Act in 1765, many American colonists decided to boycott English goods. Consequently, the Stamp Act was repealed. But in 1767, the Townshend Act went into effect. Taxes were placed on lead, glass, paint, paper, and tea. That act, too, was repealed after the colonists protested. Soon, England levied another tax under the auspices of the Tea Act of 1773. In addition to being taxed, tea could only be brought into the colonies by one company, the East India Company, and sold by government-licensed merchants. The colonists and Sons of Liberty again responded.

On November 11, 1773, the ships the *Dartmouth*, the *Eleanor*, and the *Beaver* arrived in Boston Harbor loaded with tea. The dock workers refused to unload the cargo. Governor Thomas Hutchinson, Royal Governor of the Massachusetts colony, demanded that the tax on the tea must be paid by midnight on December 16, 1773. That night more than 7,000 people gathered at Old South Church to hear speakers insist that the ships—with their cargo—go back to England. About 50 men in disguises separated themselves from the crowd and headed to Boston Harbor. They boarded the ships and dumped all 342 chests of tea into the harbor.

REVOLUTIONARY READING

Johnny Tremain by Esther Forbes (Houghton Mifflin, 1962)
The Boston Tea Party by Steven Kroll (Holiday House, 1998)
The Boston Tea Party by Richard Conrad Stein (Children's Press, 1998)

ACTIVITIES

To Throw or Not to Throw

On the night of December 16, 1773, where would your students have
been? Would they have been aboard the *Dartmouth*, the *Eleanor*, and
the *Beaver*? Would they have been part of the crowd that followed the
"Mohawks" to the harbor? Or would they have stayed at home in
protest against the Sons of Liberty's actions? Let the class form three
groups. Ask the members of each group to discuss and debate their
decisions with members from the other groups.

Was the Party a Success?

After the Boston Tea Party, the British closed Boston Harbor. No ships
could go in or out, and so no goods or supplies could leave or come
into the city. King George III also sent in more British troops to place
Boston under military control. The colonists dubbed these actions
"The Intolerable Acts." Based on this information, do students believe
that the Boston Tea Party was a success or a failure? Remind them to
explain their reasoning fully.

"I Saw the Whole Thing"

Have pairs of students take on the roles of reporters and bystanders or
participants at the Boston Tea Party. The reporters should formulate a
list of questions to ask, and be prepared to follow up answers with
more spontaneous questions; the bystanders or participants should be
ready with their version of the events. After writing their news stories, reporters should let the interviewees look them over and make
any changes. Encourage pairs to "publish" their stories for the rest of
the class to read.

Simplify the Story

Challenge students to simplify the story of the Boston Tea Party for younger readers. They can make flip books or comic books, or illustrate their own easy-to-read books. Their books can be historical fiction, from the viewpoint of a fictional character involved in the Tea Party, or a nonfiction account. Share the books with a class of younger students.

Tea Time

Where does tea come from? How is it grown and harvested? Charge students with the task of finding out more about tea; for example, where it's grown, and why; how it's harvested; different types of tea; and its history as a beverage. You may want to have groups of students collaborate on this project. Suggest that students incorporate graphs, charts, illustrations, samples, maps, folktales, or songs into their presentations.

Amazing Dioramas

Discuss the locations that were important to the Boston Tea Party—the Old South Church, the Liberty Tree under which Sam Adams and other Sons of Liberty met, the streets of Boston between the church and harbor, and Boston Harbor. Tell students to create dioramas for the locations. Have them research what Boston looked like at the time what the Sons of Liberty, other Boston citizens, and British soldiers wore and the action that occurred there. Gather a variety of materials for students to use, such as boxes, cloth, plastic soldiers and animals, yarn, paints, and so on.

1775
PATRIOTS
and
LOYALISTS

THE CHARACTERS *(in order of appearance)*

NARRATOR

Loyalists:

MERCY, age 15

HENRY, Mercy's brother, age 9

MOTHER

Patriots:

JACK, age 14

PATRICIA, Jack's sister, age 12

THOMAS, Jack's brother, age 9

Act 1

THE TIME AND PLACE
November 1775; New York City

THE SETTING
A meeting of the Ice Bears* Club in a tree house in
MERCY and HENRY'S backyard.

NARRATOR: In 1775, New York was the most important seaport on the east coast but, centered around present-day Wall Street, it was still a small town. There was plenty of open space. Kids like Mercy, Henry, Jack, Thomas, and Patricia had the room to build a tree house.

PATRICIA: Henry, I'll go if you'll go.

HENRY: But I don't want to go swimming in the winter. The water's too cold!

JACK: That's the point. The water has to be cold. We can't call ourselves the Ice Bears Club if we don't go swimming in the winter.

HENRY: Then let's call ourselves something else.

MERCY: I agree with Henry. I think it's silly. Why do we have to be ice bears?

JACK: Well, we have to be something, otherwise we don't have a club.

HENRY: I know! Let's be Loyalists.

PATRICIA: My parents are Patriots. I can't be a Loyalist. I'd rather be an ice bear.

THOMAS: I don't understand what those things are.

MERCY: Patriots and Loyalists?

THOMAS: Yes.

HENRY: I don't either.

*NOTE: The club members refer to the animal we now call a polar bear as an ice bear. The name polar bear originates in 1781, after the date of this play.

MERCY: Loyalists are loyal to England. Patriots want the colonies to leave

MERCY: Loyalists are loyal to England. Patriots want the colonies to leave England, and maybe form another country.

HENRY: Mother and Father are Loyalists, right?

MERCY: Absolutely.

THOMAS: Are our mother and father Loyalists?

PATRICIA: No, they're Patriots.

JACK: That's right. *We're* patriots.

HENRY: I thought we were all ice bears.

MERCY: The Patriots tarred and feathered Mr. Harris, the tax collector, last night.

JACK: I heard my father talking about that.

MERCY: Well, I saw it.

JACK: You *did*? You were there?

MERCY: No, but the customs house is just up the street. If I lean way out my bedroom window, I can see it.

THOMAS: What happened?

HENRY: What's tar and feather?

MERCY: They paint you with hot tar, then stick feathers on you.

HENRY: Yuck.

MERCY: Plus, it hurts.

HENRY: But why did the Patriots do that?

JACK: Because of the taxes. They're unfair. England expects us to pay taxes on glass, paper, stamps—

PATRICIA: Tea.

JACK: And the British closed the port of Boston.

MERCY: They had to do something.

JACK: Why?

MERCY: Because Patriots threw hundreds and hundreds of pounds of tea into the harbor. They were too cowardly to do it during the day, dressed as themselves. They painted their faces like Indians and sneaked onto the boats in the middle of the night.

JACK: They had rights.

MERCY: What rights? The right to destroy private property?

JACK: My father says that if the British control who we can trade with and who we can't, then they can control everything.

MERCY: England won't stand for it, and why should she? The king'll send more soldiers, and then everybody will lose their rights, all because of a few Patriots who want a revolution.

THOMAS: Revolution? What's a revolution?

JACK: It's a war in which the oppressed win their freedom from the oppressor.

HENRY: What's *oppressed* mean?

THOMAS: What's *oppressor* mean?

JACK: The British oppress the colonies by taxing us unfairly. The British are our oppressors. Got it?

PATRICIA: Oh, Jack, you sound just like Father. I don't understand why the Patriots and the British don't just sit down and talk about it.

JACK: Because the British won't listen to reason.

MERCY: Honestly, Jack. You know the Patriots keep provoking the British. The Sons of Liberty are radicals, every one of them. I'm not saying the British are perfect or even right in this tax business, but revolution? The British will never stand for it.

HENRY: But I thought we were all British.

THOMAS: Me, too.

JACK: Only as long as we want to be.

MERCY: See there? Who won't listen to reason?

HENRY: But look at us. Some of us want to be ice bears, some of us don't. That doesn't mean we should break up the club and stop being friends.

MERCY: Or burn down the tree house.

JACK: Maybe we don't have anything to talk about with the British.

MERCY: Why not?

JACK: Because we want to be our own country. Not a part of England.

PATRICIA: Instead of colonies, we would have states.

JACK: Massachusetts, New York, Virginia—

PATRICIA: Georgia, Vermont, Rhode Island—

HENRY: New Jersey, Delaware, Pennsylvania—

THOMAS: We've left some out.

JACK: North and South Carolina.

THOMAS: Georgia.

MERCY: You already said Georgia.

JACK: Maryland.

MERCY: That's only 12.

HENRY: New Hampshire!

MERCY: So the 13 colonies would become states, and those states would become a country?

JACK: Exactly.

MERCY: Suppose, say, five years from now New York decided that the new country was unjust or unfair. Would New York have the right to fight for its independence?

JACK: Well, I guess so, but—

MERCY: Would Georgia, Vermont, Pennsylvania?

JACK: I guess so, but why would they?

MERCY: Well . . . all right, take slavery.

PATRICIA: Slavery?

MERCY: My father's against slavery. He's spoken about it in church and at town meetings. What if the new country passes a law that says slavery's illegal? Some states might not agree. Then what? Wouldn't they want to become an independent country?

There is shouting from offstage.

PATRICIA: Listen!

Mercy and Henry's mother hurries onstage.

MOTHER: Mercy, Henry, where are you? I want you to come home right now!

HENRY: It's Mother! We're up here!

MERCY: She's crying! Mother, what is it?

MOTHER: Come with me! Quickly!

MERCY: What is it? What's wrong?

Mercy and Henry hurry offstage with their mother.

Act 2

THE SETTING
***Later that evening, Mercy and Henry sit glumly in the tree house.
Jack, Patricia, and Thomas enter.***

JACK: Mercy, what happened? We've been hearing the wildest stories!

MERCY: They arrested our father.

PATRICIA: Who did?

MERCY: British soldiers, that's who.

THOMAS: But I thought your father was a Loyalist.

MERCY: They kicked in our front door and took him off to jail like a common horse thief. My mother tried to stop them, but one of them pushed her down. Then my father struck the soldier, but then another one hit him in the head with his rifle butt, and they dragged him off.

PATRICIA: Oh, Mercy! Is he all right? Are you all right?

MERCY: He's home now, resting.

JACK: But *why*? Why would they arrest your father?

HENRY: They said he was a spy.

JACK: A *spy*? He's on *their* side.

THOMAS: Then how come they arrested him?

MERCY: They said they got the wrong man.

JACK: What?

MERCY: They said they made a mistake. They were looking for someone else. Can you believe that?

JACK: Can I believe the British would do something like that? Yes!

MERCY: Some Patriots came to visit him. They brought fruit and sweet-meats. Your father was one of them. They invited him to join their cause.

PATRICIA: What did your father say?

MERCY: He said he'd think carefully about it.

JACK: Listen, Mercy. This is our home. We were born here. Our parents were born here. British soldiers can't come here and kick our doors down and drag us away.

MERCY: No, no, they can't do that—but they did.

HENRY: I don't want to be a Loyalist anymore. I'm a Patriot.

MERCY (*Slowly*): You know what? I'm a Patriot, too.

THOMAS: Does this mean we're all still ice bears? Or are we Patriots now?

PATRICIA: We can be more than one thing at a time, Thomas.

HENRY: I'm still not going swimming in that cold water.

BACKGROUND
ON THE
PATRIOTS AND LOYALISTS

As a result of the Boston Tea Party, Parliament passed the "Intolerable Acts," which closed Boston's harbor until the tea was paid for, took away the right of the colony of Massachusetts to rule itself, and established military rule in the colony. Representatives from all 13 colonies met in Philadelphia in 1774 to discuss the situation. This First Continental Congress issued a Declaration of Colonial Rights and Grievances telling King George III that only the colonies had the right to impose taxes on themselves. In response, King George sent more British troops to Boston. The Second Continental Congress convened in Philadelphia in May 1775. They established a Continental Army and selected George Washington to lead it. Then the Americans and British fought at Bunker Hill and Breed's Hill. King George said that the colonies were in open rebellion and that their leaders would be hanged if caught. He also hired Hessian soldiers and sent them to America.

More and more colonists, realizing a peaceful solution with England was impossible and that a complete severing of ties with the mother country was inevitable, embraced the Patriot cause. The Loyalists, or Tories, disagreed. They wanted to continue as colonies and pledge their allegiance to the King. Tensions rose between the Patriots and Loyalists. About 80,000 Loyalists fled to Canada during the fighting, and about 50,000 aided the Redcoats as soldiers and spies.

REVOLUTIONARY READING

In the Path of War: Children of the American Revolution Tell Their Stories
   edited by Jeanne Winston Adler (Cobblestone, 1998)
The Journal of William Thomas Emerson by Barry Denenberg
   (Scholastic, 1998)
If You Lived in the Time of the American Revolution by Kay Moore
   (Scholastic, 1998)
A Young Patriot by Jim Murphy (Clarion, 1998)

ACTIVITIES

The Pros and Cons of British Rule

Discuss the advantages and disadvantages of British rule over the
colonies. Did some advantages turn into disadvantages and, if so,
how? Record students' responses in a chart on the board. Based on
their responses, how would the class rate itself—more aligned with
the Patriots or with the Loyalists?

Differing Views

Pose the following questions to students: *Have you ever disagreed with
a friend about something important? What happened? Were you able to
resolve and respect your differences? Have you experienced the same situation with someone you didn't know well? How did you deal with that situation?*

Word History

Have students use dictionaries to find the definitions and word origins
of *patriot* and *loyalist*. Ask them to draw connections among word origins, definitions, and usage of the words to describe groups of people
during the American Revolution. Challenge students to think of slang
words or nicknames for Patriots and Loyalists.

A New Ending

Suppose Mercy and Henry's father hadn't been mistakenly arrested in the play? What if the Patriots had targeted him instead for his Loyalist beliefs? Turn students into playwrights; have them rewrite Act 2 using a different incident. Can they resolve the conflicts between the Patriot and the Loyalist children, or is the rift between them too wide?

A Life-Changing Event

Which of the following events do students feel is one of the most important events in American history: Boston Massacre, Boston Tea Party, the battles at Lexington and Concord, or the battles at Bunker Hill and Breed's Hill? Have them research the events. Then direct students to take on the role of a Loyalist and to imagine how that event would strengthen or make them change their views.

Benedict Arnold on Trial

Benedict Arnold, one of Washington's most valued officers, betrayed the American cause. After the war, he moved to England and died there. Have students research Arnold and uncover the reasons for his defection to the British side. Hold a mock trial in class. Let volunteers assume the roles of Benedict Arnold, witnesses for and against Arnold, a jury, a judge, a prosecuting team, and a defense team. (You might also assign the roles yourself or have students draw slips of paper to determine which character they will play.)

1776–77
CROSSING
THE
DELAWARE

THE CHARACTERS

NARRATORS 1–2

GENERAL GEORGE WASHINGTON: *Leader of the Continental Army*

MARTHA WASHINGTON: *George Washington's wife*

Letter Writers:

PRIVATE JOHN WILLIS: *Soldier in the Virginia Militia*

LIEUTENANT GEORGE SHAW: *Officer in the Massachusetts Militia*

GENERAL CHARLES CORNWALLIS: *Officer in British army*

COLONEL ABNER GLOVER: *Officer in the Massachusetts Militia*

CALEB ROSS: *Soldier with Vermont Volunteers*

JOHN BEACHAM: *Soldier with Georgia Volunteers*

SIMON BLACK: *Soldier with Connecticut Militia*

AMERICAN SOLDIERS 1–5

AMERICAN SOLDIERS 1–10 *(nonspeaking roles)*

THE PLACE
The American Continental Army camp near the Delaware River

THE TIME
December 1776

NARRATOR 1: It's a bitterly cold winter in Pennsylvania and New Jersey along the Delaware River. On the New Jersey side of the river are 3,000 Hessian soldiers—German mercenaries hired by King George III to fight against the Americans.

NARRATOR 2: General Charles Cornwallis sent a report to the British Parliament, assuring them that the Continental Army would soon go down in defeat.

CORNWALLIS:

Report to Parliament.

Dear Sirs,

I have pursued the rebel army out of New York across the Hudson River, down the length of New Jersey, and across the Delaware River. In their flight, the Americans have burned every bridge after crossing it, felled trees in our path, and done everything to delay our pursuit.

They have temporarily evaded complete defeat at my hands by crossing the Delaware, having burned all boats remaining to me on the New Jersey side. But this measure will not save them from the snows of December. They are without shelter or warm clothing, and they have little food or ammunition. Come spring, I will sweep aside what remains of their force.

In short, gentlemen, their cause is lost.

Your Obedient Servant,

General Charles Cornwallis

NARRATOR 1: The American Continental Army camps on the Pennsylvania side of the river. The army, under General George Washington, has not won a single battle. They've been forced to retreat in the face of British advances.

NARRATOR 2: In the American camp, soldiers huddle over campfires, repair uniforms and what's left of their shoes, play cards and other games. They clean and oil their muskets. Some eat dry bread. Many,

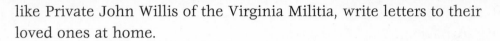

like Private John Willis of the Virginia Militia, write letters to their loved ones at home.

JOHN WILLIS:

My Dearest Wife,

 With Christmas coming on, I miss you and the little one more than I can bear. I hope the season is treating you better than it's treating us. My last pair of shoes has fallen hopelessly to pieces, but they lasted longer than most of my comrades' shoes. Now I am wearing rags tied about my feet, and I, too, leave bloody tracks in the snow along the Delaware River.

All my love,

Johnny

GEORGE SHAW:

Dear Family,

 I fear our cause is lost. We no longer even resemble a fighting army. We are a ragged band of sick and freezing men. The volunteers are deserting daily. I hate them for it, but at the same time, I understand. They have farms and families to tend, but so do I. I have no idea when or if this letter will reach you. If I should never see you again, please know how much I love you.

Your loving son and brother,

George

NARRATOR 1: General George Washington made his report to the Continental Congress.

WASHINGTON:

Honorable Members of the Continental Congress.

Dear Sirs,

 I cannot make war on our enemies without the means and materials necessary to do so. My force is spread thinly along 25 miles of the west bank of the Delaware River. They are without food, clothing, arms, and ammunition. You must supply me with these and do so quickly or, I'm sad to report, the grand ideas for which we fight will perish with us.

Yours,

General George Washington

COL. GLOVER:

My Dear Friend,

It snowed again last night. We stagger around camp like dying men. Our cause is just, but our capabilities are few. If the British—we can see their fires across the river—find boats in which to cross, we would be barely able to put up a fight. If I were the British commander, I would not attack. Why waste men when you can let the winter defeat us?

We still have all faith in General Washington, who strides about the camp like a Roman warrior doing what he can to keep up our morale, but even he cannot defeat the weather. We must do something, but I do not know what. Time presses because in the new year, the enlistments of half our army will expire, and they will leave for their homes. With them will go the last of our hopes for success.

Yours, hopefully,

Ab

NARRATOR 2: Like his soldiers, George Washington had his doubts and fears. Unlike them, he had his wife Martha with him. She stayed at the old stone house, which was Washington's headquarters at Valley Forge. Almost every day, Mrs. Washington walked among the soldiers, talking with them, passing out socks she'd knitted, mending their clothes, caring for the sick and wounded, and passing out what food she could find.

WASHINGTON: We've been retreating for six months, and if we do nothing but camp here until spring, I fear all will be lost. I must act, but how? No man, I believe, ever had greater difficulties, and less means to extricate himself from them.

MARTHA WASHINGTON: We knew it would be no easy task, taking on England. They have more resources than we do. We, however, have more to lose than they do. Our men will fight harder. They're fighting for their homes and their families.

WASHINGTON: I have in mind the beginnings of a plan. It's desperate, but so is our condition.

MARTHA WASHINGTON: Then you must act, even if acting will destroy us all and the justice of our cause.

WASHINGTON: We'll attack at dawn on the morning of December 26. The Hessians will have celebrated Christmas and, I trust, will not be rising early and on their guard. My plan hinges upon complete surprise. Without it, we cannot succeed, for I haven't the weapons or the men to risk a frontal attack.

GLOVER:

Dear Friend,

General Washington means to attack! The man has conceived a brilliant plan. He recognizes that if we remain here, the winter will defeat us. We've learned from spies that 3,000 Hessians have been stationed in Trenton across the river. This is the force that will attack us in the spring, but we're going to attack them first. I cannot send this letter, of course, for fear it would fall into enemy hands, but I am excited by the plan and couldn't sleep.

Ab

CALEB ROSS:

My Dear Sister,

The weather was dreadful on Christmas night. Sleet, snow, and wind plagued our crossing. How we struggled, how it hurt, to load our few cannons into our three tiny boats. And how we feared that river in them. The wind caused waves as on an ocean and drove ice floes into us, and capsize seemed inescapable. We knew we'd live but minutes in that freezing water.

Your brother,

Caleb

WASHINGTON: I have divided my meager force into three elements, with which I hope to surround Trenton. We will land at a point six miles north of the town, which requires my men to march in the dark over frozen roads before we can take up positions for attack. The men are outnumbered and outgunned. We have but four cannons, while our enemy has ten times that. No general in living memory has asked more from an army without shoes.

JOHN BEACHAM:

Dear Family,

    We fought cold, wind, and dreadful floes of ice, and though more than once I thought us dead, we made it across the Delaware River. However, as our little army regrouped on the bank, we discovered that many boats did not make it across the river. Did the others turn back or did they drown? We knew not. Would General Washington cancel his plans? No! He ordered us on. And we were glad. To a man we'd rather face a greater enemy than recross that terrible frozen water.

Yours truly,

John B.

SIMON BLACK:

Dear Brother,

    Only General Washington's force of 2,500 made it across the river, and I was among them. He walked among us. At over six feet tall, he towered over us like Colossus. Speaking in a near whisper, he reminded us why we fight, and what gallant souls we are to stand for liberty. I want to stand for liberty, but that night I hoped not to have to fall for liberty. It seemed likely that I would have to do just that.

Wish me well,

Simon

SOLDIER 1: By dawn, we were in position for attack. It began when we stumbled upon their sentries. Shouting and flashing our bayonets, we drove them from their posts, and we spilled into the streets of Trenton.

SOLDIER 2: Our cannon fired over our heads into the streets of Trenton. We could hear the shot ripping the air.

SOLDIER 3: We let off blood-curdling screams, muskets firing, sabers rattling. I'll tell you, my friend, we were proper terrors this Christmas Day, and I'm glad I was not on the receiving end of our wrath.

SOLDIER 4: It seemed as if the battle had raged for hours, but at the end of it, I was surprised to find that not even one hour had passed.

SOLDIER 5: I'll never forget this day for as long as I live.

NARRATOR 1: General Washington made his report to the Continental Congress.

WASHINGTON:

Honorable Members of the Continental Congress.
Dear Sirs,

It is my honor to report that we have taken Trenton, New Jersey. We attacked before dawn this Christmas Day, and took the Hessian force under Colonel Rall completely by surprise. We cut off their line of retreat, and when General Knox's artillery fired briskly down the two main streets, the Hessian officers quickly surrendered.

Without the brilliant boat handling, under very trying conditions, by Colonel Glover's Marblehead regiment, the battle could not have been engaged, let alone won.

It is my pleasure to report that in capturing 900 prisoners, 1,200 small arms, and six cannons, we lost not a single man in battle, though two brave souls froze to death en route.

Gentlemen, I beseech you, make the most of this victory and recruit MORE MEN.
Yours,
General George Washington

NARRATOR 2: General Cornwallis, who had wintered in New York City, had some explaining of his own to do.

CORNWALLIS:

Report to Parliament.
Dear Sirs,

General George Washington has taken Trenton in a diabolical sneak attack on Christmas Day. A gentleman does not wage war in winter, let alone Christmas. The General is no gentleman. He, of course, does not have the forces to hold Trenton, and when spring, the proper season for war, comes around, we will sweep him out of Trenton. However, we must recognize that this General Washington could prove a serious problem should his force grow in number.
Your Obedient Servant,
General Charles Cornwallis

JOHN WILLIS:

My Dearest Wife,

    Well, it's been quite the day. Not only am I alive, but I'm a genuine *hero*. George Washington himself said so. However, I don't know when I'll be coming home.

Soon, I hope—

John

NARRATOR 1: Many soldiers were due to leave the Continental Army on January 1 when their tours of duty were over. Each soldier was offered $10 if he would stay; almost all of them refused.

NARRATOR 2: They were tired and cold and hungry. They had promised their families they would return soon.

NARRATOR 1: Then Washington ordered the troops to parade in formation. He asked the soldiers to stay one more month. He said that he knew they had given everything they had to give–

NARRATOR 2: But they had to give a little more for liberty, and for their country. Everything depended on it.

NARRATOR 1: When it was time to ask for reenlistment, almost every soldier signed up. The war wouldn't end for another five years. There would be many more battles—won and lost—between now and then.

BACKGROUND
ON
CROSSING THE DELAWARE

IN 1776, THE BRITISH hoped to capture the important port of New York City and then use their forces to divide Massachusetts from the states to the south. Once the new nation was divided, they felt, it would surrender.

When the British general William Howe sailed to New York in June of 1776, George Washington and about 18,000 American troops were waiting for him on Long Island. Howe waited to attack until August when his 32,000 troops finally arrived. Outnumbered, the Americans had to retreat. Instead of pressing his advantage and capturing the Americans, Howe ordered his troops to rest for a day. Protected by fog, Washington and his troops were able to move north to forts that would later be named Fort Lee and Fort Washington. Washington and Howe clashed again in White Plains, New York, in October. Howe again overpowered the American forces and took both forts.

The British general Charles Cornwallis followed Washington as he retreated. The Americans burned bridges behind them as they moved south through New Jersey, and chopped down trees to block roads. In December, the Americans reached the Delaware River. They commandeered boats to take them across the river and burned any others they could find. Washington and his troops arrived safely in Pennsylvania; the British, without boats, had to camp on the New Jersey side of the river. Believing that the colonists were defeated, Cornwallis scattered his troops along the river and then sailed for England.

On the morning of December 26, 1776, when the 3,000 Hessian troops in Trenton, New Jersey, were still sleeping, Washington attacked. In less than an hour, the Americans captured Trenton.

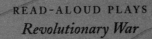

REVOLUTIONARY READING

The Winter of Red Snow by Kristiana Gregory (Scholastic, 1996)

Crossing the Delaware: A History in Many Voices by Louise Peacock (Atheneum, 1998)

Daughter of Liberty: A True Story of the American Revolution by Robert M. Quackenbush (Hyperion, 1999)

ACTIVITIES

Retreat or Stand Your Ground?

Washington retreated several times from the British army. If he hadn't, the American forces would certainly have been captured, and England would have won the war. Ask students how they feel about retreating from a confrontation. Do they consider it to be a cowardly act or a brave one? How can they put the strategy of retreating to good use in their own lives?

The United States of . . . England?

General Cornwallis was so sure that England was about to win the war that he sailed home. He was almost right. But then George Washington seized the initiative. Pose the following questions to students: *What if England had won the Revolutionary War? How do you think your lives might be different today?*

He's a Card!

Bring out the artist and the historian in your students. Have them make up a set of Revolutionary trading cards featuring people, American and British, who were important to the American Revolution. Distribute poster board, tag board, or blank index cards to students. Make sure everyone has colored pencils, markers, or paints. Ask each student to contribute at least four cards to make up a class set of cards. On the front of each card, they should draw a picture of the person, and on the back, they should briefly explain his or her contribution. Allow time for students to look at one another's cards.

Recording History

Today we can read diaries of people who lived during the American Revolution. Ask students if they think those people realized their words would still be read more than 200 years later. Did they realize they were recording history? Suggest that students start their own diaries, recording the history of their own lives and times. Which events in the community, state, nation, and world have an impact and an effect on them? Periodically, allow students to share their diaries with the rest of the class.

Fact or Fiction?

Fact or fiction—did George Washington toss a coin across the Delaware River? Challenge students to create a game called Fact or Fiction?, based on people and events of the American Revolution. Ask everyone to contribute at least five fact or fiction game cards, with answers and facts to back them up. Let students play the game in pairs, in groups, or as a class. You can be the moderator and read the cards. Students score a point for each correct answer.

The Best-Laid Plans

Washington planned a three-prong attack on the Hessians in Trenton. Unfortunately, only one third of the troops was able to make it across the Delaware River. Washington then had to divide those forces into two groups. Let groups of students draw maps of the planned attack or the actual attack on Trenton. Have groups compare the plans with what actually happened. Students may also want to draw story maps of Washington's retreat from New York City to the Pennsylvania side of the Delaware River.

1781
YORKTOWN
SOPHIE'S REVOLT

THE CHARACTERS *(in order of appearance)*

SOPHIE JAMESON: *Young girl who lives in Yorktown*

BEN JAMESON: *Sophie's brother*

MRS. JAMESON: *Sophie and Ben's mother*

THOMAS NELSON: *Older man who lives in Yorktown*

GENERAL CHARLES CORNWALLIS: *British officer*

BRITISH SOLDIERS 1–6

BRITISH SENTRY

GENERAL GEORGE WASHINGTON: *Commander of Continental Army*

COMTE ROCHAMBEAU: *French officer*

MARQUIS DE LAFAYETTE: *French officer*

BRIGADIER GENERAL CHARLES O'HARA: *British officer*

MAJOR GENERAL BENJAMIN LINCOLN: *American officer*

AMERICAN SOLDIERS 1–6

FRENCH SOLDIERS 1–6

Act 1

CORNWALLIS ARRIVES
Scene 1: July 30, 1781; The Jamesons' house, Yorktown, Virginia

SOPHIE: I'm not going. I refuse.

BEN: You can't do that, Sophie.

SOPHIE: I can, too. I'm an American. I have the right to life, liberty, and the pursuit of happiness. Going across the river to Gloucester won't make me happy.

MRS. JAMESON: You can't stay here in Yorktown by yourselves. You have to come with me. Besides, you'll have a good time.

SOPHIE: No, I won't. You'll be with Mrs. Lange, helping her take care of her baby.

MRS. JAMESON: She needs my help. Her husband's fighting with General Washington. Her baby's been sick. She's lonely.

BEN: Our father's fighting with General Washington, too.

There's a knock on the door. THOMAS NELSON enters.

NELSON: Uh-oh. Somebody's got a stubborn look on her face. What am I interrupting?

MRS. JAMESON: Sophie's exercising her rights as an American.

BEN: She's revolting.

SOPHIE: I am not!

NELSON: What are you revolting against, Sophie? Taxes? Tea?

SOPHIE: Going to Gloucester to visit Mrs. Lange and her wailing baby.

MRS. JAMESON: Just call me King George, making my children do something they absolutely do not want to do. You're both coming with me, and that's that.

SOPHIE: I'll get into all kinds of trouble in Gloucester. You'll always be telling me to stop doing what I'm doing, or looking for me, or Ben—

MRS. JAMESON: And what should I do? Leave you here by yourselves? No. I've promised Mrs. Lange, and I don't go back on my word.

SOPHIE: But—

MRS. JAMESON: That's enough, Sophie. Go upstairs and pack your things. Then help Ben pack.

SOPHIE *(Muttering):* And I thought we were fighting for *freedom* from tyranny.

MRS. JAMESON: Sophie!

Sophie and Ben exit.

NELSON: You might have your hands full with Mrs. Lange and her child and Sophie and Ben. I'm just rattling around in the house. Why don't you let them stay with me while you're gone?

MRS. JAMESON: Are you sure?

NELSON: I could use the company.

MRS. JAMESON: I don't know, Thomas. I feel uneasy with the British so close.

NELSON: Cornwallis will never come to Yorktown. It's a peninsula. It's too easy to cut him off by land and by sea. We're not a major port anymore.

MRS. JAMESON: I'll be gone for three days. Do you think you could stand it for that long?

NELSON: The longer, the better. I love having houseguests.

Scene 2: August 2, 1781; *The Nelson house, Yorktown, Virginia*

Using a telescope, Mr. Nelson looks out a window. There is the sound of shouting offstage. Sophie and Ben enter.

SOPHIE: What is it, Mr. Nelson? What's going on?

BEN: Why are all the soldiers running away?

NELSON: British ships have sailed into Chesapeake Bay. I think General Cornwallis has come to call.

SOPHIE: But why are all our soldiers running away? They should stay and fight. My father would stay and fight. So would your sons.

BEN: Maybe they're just retreating. General Washington has to retreat sometimes, and it works out for him.

SOPHIE: They're running away, they're not retreating. (*Yelling*) Cowards! Come back here and fight!

NELSON: That's enough of that, Sophie. Gather your things, quickly. Help Ben.

SOPHIE: Why? Where are we going?

NELSON: I'm taking you over to Gloucester, to be with your mother, while we can still cross the river.

BEN: But what if she's coming back here?

SOPHIE: Ben's right. What if we miss her?

NELSON: We'll just have to take the chance. Now hurry.

There's a loud knocking on the front door, then the sound of voices arguing. CORNWALLIS enters the room.

CORNWALLIS: Pardon the intrusion, Mr. Nelson. General Charles Cornwallis, here. I'm afraid you're going to be seeing quite a lot of my men and me. We're occupying your home.

SOPHIE: Oh, no you're not! You don't have the right to come in here and—

NELSON: Sophie!

CORNWALLIS: Ah, you must be one of those patriotic American fire-brands I keep hearing so much about.

SOPHIE: You're not wanted here. You should take your men and go home.

CORNWALLIS: I will, soon enough.

SOPHIE: NOW.

BEN: Yeah! Get going! NOW!

NELSON: Sophie! Ben! Being patriotic doesn't mean being rude.

CORNWALLIS: If my presence is so alarming, then you may go. I won't hold you here.

NELSON: Their mother is in Gloucester. If the children could have safe passage there . . . ?

CORNWALLIS: Certainly.

SOPHIE: I'm not leaving.

BEN: Neither am I.

SOPHIE: General Washington won't let you get away with this!

CORNWALLIS: He's hundreds of miles away in New York. I don't think your general has time to worry about what's going on here. Mr. Nelson, I'd like a bath, and then I'll have my cook prepare lunch. You and Sophie and Ben will join me, I hope?

SOPHIE: I won't!

BEN: Me neither!

They run out.

CORNWALLIS: High-spirited children. Too bad your militia doesn't have their courage, Mr. Nelson.

NELSON: I don't believe I'll be having lunch with you, sir. I must look for the children.

Act 2

THE BATTLE FOR YORKTOWN
Scene 1: September 28, 1781; British redoubt (fortress) in Yorktown

British soldiers work on fortresses. Sophie and Ben carry a lunch basket to Cornwallis.

BEN: General Cornwallis isn't so bad.

SOPHIE: Benjamin Jameson! You'd better watch what you say!

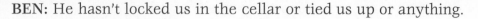

BEN: He hasn't locked us in the cellar or tied us up or anything.

SOPHIE: Just you wait.

BRITISH SENTRY: Halt! Who goes there!

BEN: Ben and Sophie, with lunch for General Cornwallis.

BRITISH SOLDIER 1: Here, let's have a look at that lunch basket. You Americans might be trying to poison our general.

SOPHIE: Poison would be too good for him.

BRITISH SOLDIER 2: Oh, I've heard about you! Sophie, the patriotic American firebrand.

Cornwallis enters.

CORNWALLIS: Ah, here you are. I was beginning to think you had run off again.

BEN: Sophie wanted to, but I—

SOPHIE: The French have scared off your warships. They've blocked Chesapeake Bay. It's only a matter of time before Washington gets here, and then you'll be sorry.

CORNWALLIS: I'm looking forward to meeting your General Washington.

BEN: Hey, what are all those sharp sticks pointing out of the fort for? It looks like a crown of sticks or something.

CORNWALLIS: They're very good for keeping the enemy away. And do you see the hole in the side? That's where we'll stick the cannons. We've got ten of these forts, all in a semicircle around Yorktown. We've got more forts further out. I'm afraid you Americans will have a hard time taking Yorktown.

SOPHIE: You shouldn't be telling us these things. We might be spies.

BRITISH SOLDIER 3 *(Laughing):* Better watch out, General sir. She might be a spy.

British Soldier 4 enters and salutes Cornwallis.

BRITISH SOLDER 4: Enemy's been sighted, sir! Marching down the road from Williamsburg! Could be 15,000 of them, or more!

The other soldiers take up their guns.

CORNWALLIS: Steady, men. Steady. Wait until they come closer. Then we'll let our cannons speak for us. Soldier, escort Miss and Mr. Jameson back to Mr. Nelson's house, please.

SOPHIE: I told you General Washington would come.

Scene 2: October 10, 1781; The Nelson house in Yorktown

There are the sounds of cannons and big guns exploding offstage. The house has been severely damaged by cannon fire. Ben, Sophie, and Mr. Nelson huddle under a table.

BEN: I wish the noise would stop!

SOPHIE: It's American noise, Ben! It's American and French cannons.

NELSON: I should have taken you over to Gloucester. Or we should have gone with everyone else and hidden in the woods or in caves.

Suddenly the noise stops. Mr. Nelson crawls to a window and looks out.

NELSON: A white flag! From the American side!

There are voices offstage. Then Cornwallis comes in.

CORNWALLIS: You're all right? Good. General Washington has asked for you. It seems he wants to knock down your house, Mr. Nelson, but not you and your guests. My men will take you as far as the town gates. We'll hold our fire until you're safely in Washington's camp.

NELSON: Thank you, sir. You're a gentleman.

BEN: I'm sorry you're on the wrong side, General Cornwallis, or I would like you.

CORNWALLIS: You and Sophie have taught me quite a lot about Americans and what they want. Miss Jameson, it was my pleasure.

SOPHIE: I'm very glad to leave you, General Cornwallis, but Ben's right. I might like you if you were on my side.

CORNWALLIS: Good luck to all of you. I doubt that we'll meet again.

Scene 3: October 17, 1781; Washington's camp outside of Yorktown

BEN: Look at your poor house, Mr. Nelson. Where do you suppose Cornwallis is staying now?

NELSON: Probably in caves, like the rest of the British officers.

SOPHIE: Do you think the guns will ever stop?

NELSON: The British aren't firing as much as before. I suspect they've about run out of gunpowder.

BEN: What happened to all those British ships that General Cornwallis was expecting from New York?

NELSON: Who knows? Maybe bad weather. Maybe there's fighting in New York.

SOPHIE: Listen!

BEN: What? I don't hear anything.

SOPHIE: Exactly! The guns have stopped.

BEN: Drumming. I hear drumming now.

SOPHIE: Look! It's a British drummer boy. There's a redcoat waving a white flag.

NELSON: A truce!

Act 3

THE BRITISH SURRENDER
October 19, 1781; a meadow outside of Yorktown

The American soldiers march in and line up on one side. The French soldiers march in and line up on the other side. GENERAL WASHINGTON and BENJAMIN LINCOLN enter and stand at one end. ROCHAMBEAU and LAFAYETTE enter and stand at the other end. Sophie, Ben, Mrs. Jameson, and Mr. Nelson stand nearby.

MRS. JAMESON: How fine General Washington looks! So tall and handsome.

BEN: Do you think General Cornwallis will see us? Do you think I should wave to him? He was awfully nice to us.

NELSON: I think you could salute him, Ben. It would be a sign of respect.

SOPHIE: Here they come. Here come the British.

There is the sound of drumming. Led by CHARLES O'HARA, the British soldiers march in. They look at the French soldiers but refuse to look at the American soldiers.

BEN: Where's General Cornwallis? I don't see him.

SOPHIE: They're ignoring us. They're refusing to look at our soldiers.

LAFAYETTE: Play "Yankee Doodle Dandy."

The Americans start to play the song. The British soldiers look at the American soldiers in surprise.

NELSON: Lafayette's taken care of that. He's forced the redcoats to look.

O'Hara turns toward Rochambeau, to surrender. Rochambeau shakes his head and points to Washington.

MRS. JAMESON: But look, the British officer's going to Rochambeau to surrender. He's turned his back on General Washington.

O'Hara goes to Washington.

O'HARA: I'm Brigadier General Charles O'Hara. General Cornwallis has taken ill. I am acting in his place.

WASHINGTON: In that case, you may surrender to my second-in-command, Major General Benjamin Lincoln.

LINCOLN: General O'Hara, your soldiers will lay down their guns, do an about-face, and march back to Yorktown.

O'HARA: Forward march! Ground arms! About face! Forward march!

The British soldiers advance. Soldier 1 throws down his gun. Soldier 2 does the same.

LINCOLN: Lay down your arms—with respect.

Soldiers 3–6 set their guns down carefully on the pile. Led by O'Hara, the redcoats march offstage. The French and Americans march out.

BEN: I feel kind of sorry for the British.

SOPHIE: What's going to happen to Cornwallis?

NELSON: Why, Sophie, I believe you like the general.

SOPHIE: I don't. I'm just feeling sorry for him for getting beaten so badly. I tried to tell him it was no use.

NELSON: She did try to warn him, it's true.

MRS. JAMESON: I can imagine. Well, let's go home, children. Let's see if there's anything left of our house.

BEN: Poor Yorktown. All full of holes and broken chimneys.

SOPHIE: Poor Cornwallis.

MRS. JAMESON: The next time I go anywhere you two are going with me—no matter what.

BACKGROUND
ON THE
SURRENDER AT YORKTOWN

*I*N SEPTEMBER 1777, the British took Philadelphia. Washington and his troops spent the winter of 1777–78 suffering at Valley Forge. Things looked bleak for the American cause. Then France joined the Americans as an ally in 1778. Hearing this news, British commander Sir Henry Clinton marched his army from Philadelphia to New York before the French navy could stop his progress. In 1780 General Charles Cornwallis began his campaign in the South. The Americans responded with hit-and-run guerrilla tactics. In the spring of 1781, Cornwallis led his troops into Virginia, then one of the richest states. That fall he and his 7,000 British and Hessian troops settled in Yorktown, a port city on a peninsula, awaiting reinforcements and supplies by sea from Clinton in New York.

Hearing of Cornwallis's location, Washington ordered the Marquis de Lafayette to cut off the neck of the peninsula so the British couldn't escape by land. Then Washington marched his own troops south to Yorktown. On the way, they met Comte de Rochambeau's soldiers. Their combined forces totaled 16,000 men. Another 3,000 men on board a fleet of French warships sailed into Chesapeake Bay. British escape by water was now blocked.

For eight days, from October 9 to October 18, the Americans and French bombarded the British forces with heavy artillery. With ammunition running low and no reinforcements in sight, Cornwallis surrendered. Although there was more fighting, the battle at Yorktown effectively ended the war. On March 5, 1782, the British Parliament voted to begin peace negotiations with the Americans. A peace treaty between the two countries was signed in Paris, France, on September 3, 1783.

REVOLUTIONARY READING

The World Turned Upside Down by Richard Ferrie (Holiday House, 1999)

A Message for General Washington by Vivian Schurfranz (Silver Moon, 1998)

Songs and Stories from the American Revolution by Jerry Silverman (Millbrook, 1994)

ACTIVITIES

Compete and Cooperate

American and French forces fought together at Yorktown. George Washington urged both armies "to compete for honor, cooperate for victory." What do students think Washington meant? Is it good advice? Is it something they can use, or have used, in their own lives? If so, ask students to explain.

Negotiating for Peace

On March 5, 1782, the British Parliament voted to begin negotiations for peace with the Americans. A peace treaty was finally signed in Paris, France, on September 3, 1783. Assign students to the English or the American peace negotiating team. Ask each team to think about what it wants—and thinks it can get. Then have the teams meet to discuss the terms of peace.

News from the Front

Have students take on the roles of roving reporters during the battle at Yorktown. Assign one day of the battle—from September 28, when the Continental Army first arrived in Yorktown, to October 19, when the British laid down their arms—for each student to report on. You may also let students work together in pairs or groups to report on several days' events. Suggest that they consult various sources such as diaries, biographies, and fiction and nonfiction works. Ask the class to think of a name for their newspaper and design a masthead. If possible, ask students to "print" their articles using a computer.

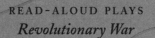

Revolutionary Websites

Ask students to survey Internet websites that focus on some aspect of the American Revolution. For instance, *www.PBS.org/ktca/liberty/* offers details of the surrender at Yorktown, games, and links to other related topics. Have students write reviews of the websites, including content, links, and ease or difficulty of using the site.

What Ever Happened to . . . ?

What ever happened to the British, French, and German officers who fought against and with the Americans during the Revolutionary War? Did participating in the war change their lives? What ever happened to General Charles Cornwallis? Baron Friedrich von Steuben? Marquis de Lafayette? Jean Baptiste Donatien de Vimeur, Comte de Rochambeau? Sir Henry Clinton? Ask students to find out what happened to these men after 1781 and to write reports on them.

The Stories Behind the Songs

Tell students to research songs that were popular during the American Revolution, especially those that were written about specific events. You might challenge them to investigate whether or not the song "The World Turned Upside Down" was actually sung at the British surrender at Yorktown. Have students bring in copies of songs—and musical instruments—and let the class perform and discuss the songs.